JAAN KAPLI. ... ly after the
Soviet occupa ... an, but his
father, who dis ... ...rthern Russia
while the poet ... ...ied there, was Polish. "My
childhood," he h ... passed in Tartu, a war-devastated univer-
sity town. It was a time of repression, fear, hypocrisy and poverty."
Kaplinski studied Romance Languages and Linguistics at Tartu
State University and has since been a student of anthropology,
especially of the works of Paul Radin, Claude Lévi-Strauss, and
the linguist Benjamin Whorf, as also of Mahayana Buddhism,
and of the philosophies of the Far East. His poetry has gained him
a reputation as one of Eastern Europe's most gifted poets. He is
also an essayist and professor, with several prose works published
in his homeland. He has translated from Spanish, French, English,
Polish and Chinese, and co-translated his own poems (with Sam
Hamill and Riina Tamm) for the two earlier collections, *The Same
Sea in Us All* (1990) and *The Wandering Border* (1992). He is also
the author of *I Am the Spring in Tartu* (1991), a book of poems
written in English and published in Canada. After Estonian
Independence in 1991, he became for a time an MP in the
Estonian Parliament (1992–5). He lives in Tartu with his wife and
children, writing columns for newspapers and giving lectures in
several universities in Estonia and in Finland.

HILDI HAWKINS is a writer, editor and translator. She studied
mathematics at the University of Edinburgh and musicology at
the University of Helsinki. She is co-editor of the literary maga-
zines *Books from Finland* and *transitions*, and editor of *things*, a
journal of writings about objects, their histories and meanings.
Her recent publications include *On the Border: New Writing from
Finland* (co-edited with Soila Lehtonen; Carcanet, 1995) and a
translation of the Finnish writer Leena Krohn's *Doña Quixote and
Other Citizens and Gold of Ophir* (Carcanet, 1995).

Other books by Jaan Kaplinski
available in Harvill editions

THE SAME SEA IN US ALL
THE WANDERING BORDER

Jaan Kaplinski

THROUGH
THE FOREST

*Translated from the Estonian
by Hildi Hawkins*

THE HARVILL PRESS
LONDON

First published in Estonian with the title *Tükk elatud elu*
by Eesti Kostabi Selts, Tartu, 1991

First published in Great Britain as *Through the Forest* 1996
by The Harvill Press
84 Thornhill Road
London N1 1RD

First impression

This translation was published with the financial support of
the European Commission

A CIP catalogue record for this title is
available from the British Library

ISBN 1 86046 198 0

Designed and typeset in Bembo at
Libanus Press, Marlborough, Wiltshire

Printed and bound by Butler & Tanner
at Selwood Printing, Burgess Hill

CONTENTS

THROUGH THE FOREST

to my "friend"
with love

There is so little that remains: the handful of last year's snow
that I squeezed in my hand as we skied, the three of us,
toward Kvissental across the peat pond.
The wind in the heather between Viki and Audaku.
The scent of St John's wort and marjoram tea in Aruküla in the
    early morning.
The titmouse that flew into the stove and was burnt to death.
A couple of folk songs, a wooden spoon,
the cockerel on St John's church and a little piece of black bread,
we do not even know when and where from. What do they have
    in common?
We do not know that, either. Between the great fingers of the
    twilight,
which slowly close tight around us,
a few tiny crumbs sometimes fall. Something of us.
Something of the world. Something that remains undiscovered.
Goes on falling. We do not know where from, we do not know
    where to.

To eat a pie and to have it – I
sometimes succeed – I exchange
a piece of lived life for poetry, and then on
for roubles and kopecks – I live off that same
life, eat my own tail and shins
and they grow again, always anew
and the eagle of poetry rises again into flight
and tries to rise with me away from this world
toward a higher world, from which, once,
I was expelled. I remember it
and in my dreams I see it over and over again,
but in reality I do not know how to go there,
although I go on reading stories and folklore studies,
believing that one day I shall discover the way.
Then I shall still need wings. Only wings.
Perhaps my own.

I watch your determination: you make of your life
an austere architecture. Floor by floor
you rise higher. A chequered row of windows
glinting in the glow of sunset. But one of them,
on the very highest floor, is ajar
and from it, into the gathering twilight, gazes
a soul – in its nightdress, hair tousled, eyes crazed,
clenched in its mouth as yet uncertain
a cry for help or a scream: 'Go away!'
or 'Don't leave me alone!'
Or both at the same time.

Lines do not perhaps exist; there are only points.
Just as there are no constellations, only stars
which we combine into water carriers, fish, rams,
virgins, scorpions and ourselves.
Points are of themselves, lines of us.
Lines are not real. Constellations, contours, profiles,
outlines, ground plans, principles, reasons,
ulterior motives and consequences . . .
A solitary birch holds onto its last leaves by the woodshed.
Or the leaves hold onto the birch.
Or there is someone who holds onto them both,
like a child holding his father's and mother's hands at once.
I am sorry for them – the child, the leaves, the father, the
    birch and the mother.
But I do not know, really, for whom: if the birch exists,
if there are only points. I do not want the winter.
But I do not know whether the winter really exists.
    There are only points.
There are only molecules and atoms, which move
    increasingly slowly,
which is roughly the same as saying: warmth disperses
throughout space. Both the child's hands were cold.
Night is coming – light is roughly the same as warmth.
Light scatters in the empty room. New thoughts
come so seldom. Your hand is warm. So is the night.
The poem is ready. If the poem exists at all:
there are only points. It is dark.

As the night begins, a forked birch captures
the light of a streetlamp and is as bright
as the nameless star that shines between its branches.
The snow remains in darkness, the snow slips the mind,
only the birch does not go, does not stay, and the star
in the dark sky, and the child who slithered
all the way home from school, slid, fell down
and got up again. But the snow slips the mind,
in the snow's place is empty space, but it is perhaps
this which makes breathing so light
and the sky so deep.

I begin to wash my son's shirt. In the pocket I find a piece
   of paper.
On it:
   2: 06 27
   An hour ago winter began. Now we are speeding toward
   summer at 30 km/s. The sun is reflected in the window.
The washing is done. I come out. Under the Christmas tree,
   all the children's animals are gathered in bunches: the tiger,
   the lion, six dogs, two bears, a squirrel, a beaver, two cats,
   a lizard and someone else besides.
Just as in the prophecy of Isaiah, in which 'the wolf shall dwell
   with the lamb, and the lion shall eat straw like the ox'.
I would then eat fresh bread and grapes.
Fresh bread and grapes, and and in the evenings a little garlic.
What is the weather like now in Palestine? What is in flower
   there now?
I go to catch the bus. I stand by the roadside beside the hawthorn
   hedge and break off a
long thorn.
As a toothpick.
There are still a few frozen berries on the bush.

Think back to the vanished day
from which you are separated by sleep, restless, erotic.
Think, remember, find yesterday's own face,
so that you will not be lost in oblivion, will not be lost
among similar faces, amid time
that has passed only in activity,
walking, talking, searching the shops for
a jacket or a desk, getting angry because
the table is so difficult to put together,
some bolts are damaged and there are none
in reserve − economic policy at screw level,
since at the same time metal is simply dug into the ground
by the ton − all of this creates
a background of irritation to the everyday, just like clouds,
through which so few things can reach,
a fresh thought, a fresh glance, a woman's or a child's
laugh, you note what gives even the day
most of the way it looks − the look of a living person,
you make contact, you are together, you draw
with a coloured pencil, Lemmit and Elo-Mall
draw too and when they ask what is it
you're drawing you say, oh, nothing much.

Once, at a meeting, I was asked
to describe a poet's day. So
I did:

> I get up and make porridge for the children.
> I take one child to school or study at home with the other.
> I take the other child to school.
> I go to the grocer's shop.
> I meet some friends in the town.
> I talk on the telephone at home.
> I do the laundry.
> I clean the room.
> I read a newspaper.
> I write a little.
> I make food for someone.
> I eat.
> I put one child in the bath and then settle it for sleep.
> I make the bed.
> I lie down.
> I discuss the day's news with my wife.
> If I am not very tired, I read.
> . . . .

It was like this, or a little different.
It is like this, or a little different.

Death does not come from outside. Death is within.
Born-grows together with us.
Goes with us to kindergarten and school.
Learns with us to read and count.
Goes sledging with us, and to the pictures.
Seeks with us the meaning of life.
Tries to make sense with us of Einstein and Wiener.
Makes with us our first sexual contacts.
Marries, bears children, quarrels, makes up.
Separates, or perhaps not, with us.
Goes to work, goes to the doctor, goes camping,
to the convalescent home and the sanatorium. Grows old,
sees children married, retired,
looks after grandchildren, grows ill, dies
with us. Let us not fear, then. Our death
will not outlive us.

The wind does not blow. The wind is the process of blowing itself.
Can there be wind that does not blow? Sun that does not shine?
A river that does not flow? Time that does not flow.
For time is flux. But no one knows what it is that
flows. Or can there suddenly be
time that waits, that remains in one place like the lake
behind the dam? Can there be fire that has not yet
begun to burn, that has not even begun to glow?
Can fire be cold? Can lightning not yet have struck?
Thoughts not yet be thought? Can there be life
that is not yet lived and will perhaps remain
an empty space, a black hole in a dry witches'-broom,
a wave that freezes before it reaches the shore and now
gazes at me from the edge of the table
and knocks at my heart in my sleep?

You step into the morning, which every day grows
darker and darker. Two silent shapes
disappearing into the garage – the last I see of you.
Sleep will no longer come. The radio is playing music
which is as grey as the weekday morning.
Now you have already driven off, now turned on the headlights,
now you begin to move, reach the main road,
to flow with the sparkling flow of cars going to work and school,
you disappear beyond a curve and all that remains of you
is an image and belief and trust that you will come back,
and love, which may be greater yet,
still greater perhaps than the dark grey which is becoming light grey
in the yard, in the house, and in us.

The ticking of the clock fills the room.
Time conquers the room. Time and darkness,
in which you hear your own breathing, your eye-
lids' untiring open-shut, open-shut
and – more than you would think – the beating of your heart,
life's own biological clock, lub-dub, which is much older
than tick-tock, much closer to time itself,
time, which perhaps, really,
is something more than ticks and tocks,
is the voice of someone who has for two billion years
been wanting to say something to you, to life or to matter.
Perhaps this is the answer, one letter,
one syllable in an answer which, after two billion years,
is about to be completed.

A flock of jackdaws on the outskirts of the town – in the twilight
fluttering hither and thither in the wind and rain,
tearing apart like an old grey tea towel,
a cloth forgotten in the washing-place in the yard
where in the rain, snow and sun
it slowly rotted, moved from the man-made world back into nature
and in the spring, when we tried to wipe our hands on it
it fell into shreds on the sprouting grass.
It, too, returns, only in a different form, as something else
and it is much more difficult to recognize than the grey birds
that, each evening, fly to the trees in the graveyard for the night
and, each morning, fly to the town and to the dumping ground
and one day, too, will decompose and meet
the old tea towel and last year's newspapers,
tin crowns from the Estonian time, Rinaldo Rinaldi and Tarzan,
me and you and all the encounters, passings-by,
which can somehow take on the appearance of you and me and
        the flock of jackdaws
and the tea towel and the tin crown and the twilight.

On the border between recognition and understanding,
sometimes this side, sometimes that, sways J. K.
in the autumn wind, like the dry stem of a meadowsweet.
When he writes, on the far side of the border of intelligibility.
When he makes porridge, washes the clothes or washes his face,
presumably on the near side. Close to the border
measurements, distances and qualities alter.
Things get mixed up, soap doesn't lather,
water boils at room temperature, ice doesn't melt,
ermine stay white in summer and art seems so artistic
that J.K. wants to write himself free of art,
write himself free of himself. Everything around him
becomes ever more distant – newspapers, children, books,
everything becomes less his own; the distant
is even clearer and sharper, while what is close by
becomes hazy, books difficult to read, and what is closest of all
dissolves completely, so
you point your finger and probe the part of the room
where your body or soul should be,
but there's no trace of either.
Presumably poetry has reached its goal.

Cedar nuts and bark on the table in a Japanese cup,
an ant walking along the windowsill – they fell in
to the cyclamen pot that stood in the summer garden in the
    country
in the shade of the briar rose – and in that pot
they now, probably, live, perhaps until spring,
a pinch of ants going about their business
on the nursery window, climbing up the curtains and the
    flowerpots,
where a couple of dark-red flowers rise toward the light.

I do not write, do not make poetry, about summer, about
    autumn,
about winter or about spring, about nature or about people.
I write about writing, about making poetry itself.
I am writing a poem, although I don't know how,
I really don't – if I did, I would do it all the time,
I would know beforehand what I will write, but I don't know.
    What comes, comes,
and sometimes does not come at all. I don't know what it is
what (or who) brings to mind its beginning,
whether bird or butterfly, woman or child or word,
something you notice and see more clearly than at other times.
That I don't know how to do either, sometimes it simply works.
I can't direct my own eyes or mind, I don't know
who or what directs them. What directs noticing,
understanding. If there's something I can do, perhaps it's
observing that observation, grasping that seeing.
If that's knowledge; perhaps it's the opposite.
Perhaps, after all, poetry comes entirely from ignorance,
is a particular sort of ignorance. And that
is much harder to learn than knowing.

The chair you sit on, the flower at the window, the sheet of
     paper on the table,
the pencil in your hand, your hand itself, you yourself – all
disappears, melts, loses its outline,
unless you are able for a few moments
to follow it, without eye or thought
suddenly jumping sideways or forward. Something exists
solely because you don't really notice it.
Absent-mindedness gives things a clear form. Attention
opens the door to a completely different kind of world
where nothing is itself, where everything is in everything
and everything is something else, as I have long suspected
and also written a couple of times. And of which
almost fifty years ago, Gunnar Ekelöf wrote,
as I have just discovered:

> The only thing that exists
> is something else!
> The only thing that exists
> in this thing that exists
> is something else!
> The only thing that exists
> on this thing that exists
> is the thing that in this thing
> is something else!

Thus I, too, am part of something which, for Ekelöf,
was something else. That we have in common. Q. E. D.

I never weary of looking at leafless trees. Poplars,
lindens, birches – everything that can be seen
from my window. I do not know what it is in them that is at once
so strange and intolerably beautiful, so that I always want
to do something, want to draw them,
or describe them, although I do not know how.
I do not know, either, how to describe what I feel
as I sit at the window and watch the swaying of the branches
in the growing twilight, a few crows
in the top of the old ash, the birch in front of the woodshed.
I simply write about them, name them:
Populus, Tilia, Betula, Ulmus, Fraxinus,
as some read mantras, some name saints.
And I feel better. Perhaps I even know
that in those treetops, branches, in that ordinary,
windy pattern, drawn in black on grey,
is something much more. As in the hollow of one's hand:
Nature. Fate. The future. The poplar's character.
The birch's fate. The linden's temperament. It is very hard
to explain in words. Without words
it is hardly easier. The worlds of people
and of trees are so different. But still,
there is something so human, almost intelligible,
in that tangle of branches. It is like a script,
like a language that I do not understand, although I know
that what is written there
has long been known to me; it cannot be much different
from what can be read in books,
hands or faces.

The children are away from home. Absent, for once,
 their incomprehensible fears and jealousies
their incessant struggle for their mother's attention.
The children are away, other sounds return
gradually to the house: creaks, rustles, rattles.
Silence itself gradually takes on a different tone,
becomes deeper and more profound. Frightened
 thoughts
take their heads from under their wings, stretch and
 look round
as if thinking (he writes that thoughts think!)
whether to take flight for a moment, to go
 wandering
and achieve something great and proud
or to take the opportunity and simply dive
into this silence of home-spacetime,
flow with this murky winter day
and in this flowing rediscover
window, door, walls, ceiling, shadows and light,
my own body and my absent wife and children
somewhere in the same town in the light of the same
 winter day.

How well the crow suits this November landscape
as it caws in the leafless apple tree. The magpie
hopping in the half-stacked pile of birch logs. Black–white–grey
everywhere. Only the titmouse and the bullfinch,
only a tiny patch of blue glimpsed for a moment
between the low clouds, to recall that
colours do still exist,
although most of them have faded,
crumbled, flown away, become dream islands,
everlasting heather-flowers, which close
above the writer's tired head.

The most disconsolate of landscapes – a beach in autumn,
leafless brushwood, full of scraps of plastic, tin cans, condoms.
Lopsided changing rooms, a crow's tracks
by the water's edge on the wet sand, snails' shells,
leafless branches, sodden roots
and everywhere the low low sky and clouds
rushing as if they were in a hurry
to get somewhere far away before the dark,
which has never really disappeared, which is always
in the same place between the bushes, billowing before your eyes,
eying you; which presses on your temples
like a damp hand. And still, in all this,
there is so much unintelligible light, and you cannot tell
whether it is shining from the outside in, or the inside out,
whether it is white or black or something completely different.

Poems have lived on the earth since the Eocene age. Their ancestors lived mostly in forests and savannahs.

With the general cooling of the climate, one species accommodated itself to the severe conditions of the tundra.

The skin of the poem is thick, almost hairless, covered in wrinkles. The weight of an old poem can reach 7.5 tons, its shoulder height 4 metres.

In spite of its massive physique, the poem is astonishingly agile, with light movements, swift, but not hurried.

It swims superbly, can climb a steep bank without noticeable effort, feels itself to be at ease on the rocks.

Poems together in the forest are a remarkable sight.

Noiselessly they crowd into the thicket, as if cutting through it.

It is as if they were immaterial: no crackling, no rustling, no movement of branches or leaves.

Poems seldom live alone. The assemblies where, at various times, they gather themselves together, which have been described through the centuries by travellers, are today generally not to be found.

More than half a century ago, poem-hunting was officially banned, reservations were set up and the poem was saved.

Unfortunately, little space was left to it, but it can nevertheless feel calm only on its reservation.

People derive great benefit from the poem. Without poetry, life would lose itself in its own glamour. The entire nature, behaviour, of poetry is to feel profound peace, dignity, latent power.

Involuntarily you feel for those giants, those witnesses of long-past times, respect, sympathy, and even inspiration.

From the outside, ideals look rather like rabbits, tailless marmots or great big calling hares. The snout is short, with a split upper moustache, the ears small, some species are covered almost completely with fur;

the legs are short but sturdy. The four-toed foreleg has flattened claws that look like a hoof. The back legs have three toes.

On the bare soles pads are found, but with the help of certain muscles and supported by the substrate of the limb, the centre of the arch of the sole may be raised. A vacuum is thus created, and the foot sticks firmly to rock or to the side of a tree trunk. Such an adaptation enables ideals rapidly and skilfully

to run along vertical rock-faces and tree-trunks, upwards and downwards. They breed throughout the year. Gestation lasts 7 to 7.5 months.

Newborn ideals are well-developed, can see, and are covered in fur. They rapidly become independent. Young ideals are likeable and easily

tamed; when fully grown, however, they are savage and aggressive.

SILENCE. DUST

I

In the beginning is no beginning.
In the beginning is silence. Silence is within you. You dare not
    touch it prematurely – no one dares.
It is not worth being a 'poet' – writing poems, unless you
    cannot do otherwise – if you can, leave them unwritten.
Silence and light.
Bright silence, beneath which those words exist. Images.
    Pictures. Poetry.
Mouse nests. Spiders. Ticks. Queen bees. Clumps of grass.
The world under the clumps.
Albrecht Dürer and Harry Martinson. Dreaming forever of
    what they saw,
from which they got their picture or poetry. A clump with
    violets. Clumps – *Tuvor*.
Artist and poet hibernating in their own creation,
covered by written and unwritten pages.
Yet paper remains white rather than mottled, patterned,
    written upon.
Individual letters are like freckles, they don't change anything
    much.
The bright silence remains. Snow, and beneath the snow ice,
    and under the ice a current, quivering, arrowheads and
    spring moss.
Mouse tracks in the snow, which the wind wipes away. Snow
    dust spinning
over the emptiness, a couple of milkweed leaves and pieces of
    pine bark.
A couple of words. Laconic, far eastern, almost wordless
    wordsmanship.
White silence. An actor's white make-up, beneath which, deep
    in the darkness, the face and the soul with their own
    passions.
A throaty song, a song that comes from the stomach, from a
    person's centrepoint, his deepest part, his Marianas trench.

2

Wherever there is silence, dust gathers.

Dust wants peace. Dust gathers where there is little movement.

Dust comes

from near and far, from roads, ploughs, old fur coats, volcanoes and outer space.

Dust comes and settles on piano lids in arts centres, old Bibles in attics, shelves, rugs, laundries, smithies, abandoned mills,

in old outbuildings where old wooden bowls stand, yarn windles, dismantled looms and chests full of balls of rags.

I, too, want peace. That is why I encounter dust so often. I love to visit laundries, smithies, abandoned mills and old outhouses.

I believe that time moves more slowly there, and thoughts or images or whatever one should call them sink in slower time slowly to the ground.

Sometimes onto this paper here, and so sometimes they can be called writing, a text.

Before time breaks in the doors and something remains hopelessly unfinished,

the castle in the air unbuilt, the train of thought unspun, the mind unclarified.

Only over paper does time not have great power.

Sometimes something remains there.

Like, for example:

3

Peace conquers everything.
Peace hoists the flag of peace
over chimney, sauna, garden,
campfires, Pond Hill,
where once the Southern and Northern Kingdoms
waged war all summer long.

*

All is full of peace,
car, outbuilding, sauna, shed, byre, privy,
beehives, nesting boxes, bath, washbasin,
ash bucket, wheelbarrow, flowerpots, paint tins,
baskets, barrels, pockets and plates.

My own disquiet no longer
finds a place to be,
there is no longer room for it anywhere
except in words;
my restlessness can
now exist only
in heart and poetry.

Poetry is an extension of the heart,
an extension of its beating
into trees, bushes,
apple blossom, scarlet grosbeaks,
spider's thread, clotheslines.

4

PEACE

is when everything slowly grows its roots,
this old outbuilding, this greenhouse,
this rhubarb bush, which I planted the day before yesterday,
this old iron, this old samovar,
those little vases Tiia made,
this empty matchbox,
this figure carved from limewood,
this pebble, brought from Saaremaa, full of fossilized snails'
    shells,
this *kantele*, which we found in an empty house,
this little mouse, which runs under the loom from one wall to
    the other,
this spider, which waits on the dusty windowpane,
this old, white button on the windowsill,

this fork, which came to light as we dug the garden,
these apple trees, those garden posts, those laths, those trellises,
those wall logs, dead these sixty years,
those shingles, which we cut at the Sahkri sawmill —
all these are gradually growing roots.
I, too.

5

The spider has sucked dry
one more fly.
Life-sap changes owner.
The affinity of everything for everything,
the war of everything against everything,
the great festival of creation
in which everything is, in turn,
the eater and the eaten
and what succeeds in escaping
sinks into the sand or the mire
and eventually becomes coal
and instead of burning
in someone's innards
it burns in a central heating furnace
one February afternoon,
when the titmouse sings for the first time
and the red sun begins to set
in the southwest behind the radar and the forest.

6

The white wagtail flies
in the wind to the swaying wire,
finds its balance
and sings its brief, passionate song.
The rain has stopped for a moment,
only
here and there, from the leaves of an apple tree,

a few drops fall and, caught by a drop,
a few white petals fall
down onto the black peat heap.

7

The cuckoo, the clock of springtime,
behind the marsh in the birch grove:
tick-tock
cuck-oo
strikes, as if with an axe,
shavings from the side of time.
My son makes a boat
and cuts his finger again.
The drop of blood marks
the present moment,
the moment of free fall
when all are equal –
the stone and the feather,
the beggar and the king,
the gnat and the poet,
the yarn windle and the bootjack.
The future – a great black hole
in a black void.
I do not see it,
do not feel its weight.

8

The rain is like the centipede
who began to think
how it is he walked
and could not continue his journey.

Again and again the drops fall
onto the same
flowers, leaves, twigs,

but the sun moves on
somewhere in the upper air.

Looms and shadows
stand still,
the spider in its net-corner
and the whistle in the mouth of the warbler.
Only thought moves
and the gooseberries swell
against the autumn
which one can still say is
far off.

It is good that one's eyes
do not look backward
inside oneself
and that grey hairs
are no heavier to bear
than black ones.

9

Three spiders
have divided between them
the four panes of the window,

the transparent landscape,
in whose background
in the third dimension
the apple tree blossoms
and the leaves of the snowberry
palpitate under the rain-
drops.

On the windowsill
a pair of dried wings.
One dried butterfly.

On the other side of the garden, behind the streaming rain,
on the wall of the room
tick the grandfather clock and the electricity meter,
never catching each other up.

The radio is still playing
Schubert's unfinished symphony,
the voice of the rain fills the pauses,
the silence the voice of the rain.
No one knows where they come from.
No one knows where they go.

But we are ourselves
differently from music,
differently from the rain.
For we do not, really, live –
life lives in us
like fire in a burning field
leaping from stem to stem.

Perhaps somewhere someone
is turning a cornfield into an assart,
sowing seeds in the ashes.
But that
is already beyond my understanding.

11

What, after all, can I write?
About what was – memories.
About what could come to be – dreams.

I do not want either.
I want to write
above all about what is.

About the present. But the present is
the meeting of two walls – the very same
memories and dreams. And between them
is only a corner, too tight
to write in it, *it is*.

Now I understand:
I stand once more in the corner
as once in University Street
and want to believe that from there
from that elusive line
a door opens to somewhere else
somewhere far away.

12

When you write, you have died a little.
If you want to write about life
it is difficult to grasp it
and live.
You have stepped away from life:
instead of living, you write;
if you want to be honest,
you must write about writing,
about how you write instead of living,
about how you write about
how you write instead of living,
the same again here, the same again
about the same again.
You want to draw a line through everything
which would lead to that same
nonexistent present
point.
In the belief that through the point
passes yet another line, the door to
the other side.

In the old outbuilding
where I sit at an old table
and where there is suddenly
so much silence and space.

13

Go, go, says the easing rain.
Away, away, says the easing rain.
A petal from the apple tree falls onto the grass.
Beauty cuts deeply like a knife,
cuts the personality into many pieces.
One self thinks suddenly of November,
of the first snow, which is
like an old lady's clean white net curtain,
only on the other side of the window.
A second self thinks of tiredness,
of how the garden is tired, the house is tired,
the bushes are tired, the flowerbeds are tired,
you yourself are tired, tired of life, existence,
expectation, of getting up and going
into that tired world.
But a third self suddenly realizes:
sometimes one can also grow tired of being tired.

When I open the door, raindrops are no longer
falling from the sky. In the southwest the sun glimmers
through a thin cloud. Water drips from the eaves,
but one large bee
is already spinning out from under the outhouse eaves.
I put on my rubber boots and realize
that the world is at the same time
very old and very young
and I myself am neither.

THE FOREST FLOOR

I

The wind blows high above.
Below, under the birch trees and the raspberry canes
the dusk grows gradually
from which anonymous birds
launch into flight
and disappear into the thicket.

The summer builds, in the timber frame,
a multistoreyed postmodern house
whose inhabitants
do not really know one another.

Seldom does he who lives under the tussock
meet the resident of the tree top.
The ecological thread
which binds everything to everything else
is too long
and too fine.

You come here – you are a stranger.
Here, different laws and relationships hold good.
We may have christened them, but that does not concern them,
they do not know it.
Linnaea borealis knows nothing of Carolus Linnaeus.
It just grows.

Three pine trees, grown together.
You lean against one of them – the trunk is still warm.
The cooling of the air has not yet reached them,
although the stones are already chilled.

A solitary, sickly, congealing gnat
takes its opportunity and lands on the back of your hand.

2

A pile of stones.

Slowly covered by twigs, leaves and moss, until all that is left of it is a mound.

Each stone has its own face, its own colour.

Perhaps they have names and personalities, too, but they are so slow.

Perhaps 11,000 years – about how long it is since the retreating glacier left them here – is not enough for them to gain a clear idea of their identity, to realize their own individuality, their separation from the grey womb of the Northlands from which they were once pulled forth.

We may say we are one with creation, but do we really understand what it means.

We are intruders here, we are very far from those who are at home here.

Like the wood horsetail, which spreads its soft sunshade over the rotting leaves.

Like the wood sorrel, whose flowers are as sour as its leaves.

Like the bilberry, which by springtime has forgotten everything, whose young naïve sprigs are full of optimism and curiosity.

Like the lingonberry – dark and solemn, Juhan Liiv-like, Paul-Eerik Rummo-like, which remembers everything and dares not rise too high,

the lingonberry, the real master, who moves to the forest when the forest is ready.

But *Linnaea*, the twinflower, has begun to move.

I guessed it long ago, I noticed it first.

The twinflower is enlarging its territory, it advances about half a metre a year.

Perhaps its speed will gradually grow – I do not know.

In any case, it has plenty of time, and it will be difficult for anyone to try to keep it from advancing.

I believe it intends to conquer the whole world – which perhaps does indeed belong to it.

3

For a couple of days we all ate young spruce tips, so that our mouths became tender.

And so the summer is at hand.

On the road, by the ditch, a couple of burnt stones from our sauna have crumbled to sand.

On the path grow rushes: a couple of patches of dark, stiff green – like pieces of old horsehair mattress.

At the edge of the forest, in the middle of a footpath, a solitary strawberry blooms, its flower turned toward the south, toward the sun and the open country.

In the dike a stream murmurs and grows spring moss.

Around the forked birch is grass, full of cowslips, like brass key-blanks in a locksmith's drawer.

Which is the true key of the sky?

Blue moor grass and bird's-eye primroses together, as if they were well acquainted with the work of Lippmaa and others on plant association in Estonia.

Amid the ruins of a hay barn between the nettles and the meadowsweet, a solitary dandelion blooms, this year for the first time.

Beauty scratches, like a puppy at a door – when it gets out, it wants in, when it gets in, it wants out –

so that it no longer knows which side it is on,

does not know which is the most painful and essential of all,

the yearning to see it all to the core, to crawl free of oneself, to crumble to dust in all those sky-keys, bird's-eye primroses, rushes, nettles and dandelions

or to scoop them together, whether in photographs, poems or memories, store them up, pass them on to someone who is in need of them

and feel how he begins to come alive again,

to sense the scent of young nettles and streams and the touch of the evening breeze

as I step over the river marsh toward the forest.

THROUGH THE FOREST

I have sometimes wanted to escape. To go away, without anyone seeing or knowing.

As in childhood, when I crept under the blanket in the big bed and pretended to be a badger or a fox.

Or sat quiet in the wardrobe and imagined that no one would ever find me, that I was lost forever, but existed all the same.

So I have attempted at once to exist and not exist, which perhaps we all want, but which it seems very few of us are able to do.

We want to exist, but without bearing the burden of existence, to be disembodied and carefree,

to see, but remain unseen, to hear, but remain unheard, to fly with the wind and to pass through walls and rocks.

Since we cannot do it ourselves, we have let the characters in fairy tales exist nonexistently instead.

*

Sometimes this does not help. Sometimes it is necessary to go. To the forest or the sea or even the shed loft or the old sauna. I go to the forest.

But I also want to write. About all I do and see.

I know that I shall return, my escape is a ritual, it is suicide in a doubly metaphorical sense.

I put a small black notebook and ballpoint pen in my jacket pocket. I think: I have two possibilities – at the one extreme, to write about everything, which would mean I had no time for anything but writing (then, too, there would hardly be anything to write about), or to write about nothing at all, which offers opportunities to do everything without hindrance. Writing gets in the way of living and walking. I must make a compromise. I walk and look: if I see something significant, then after a moment I stop and write.

*

I open the gate. The post is rotten and wobbles. There is no one in sight. Tiia and Elo-Mall are weeding the strawberry patch in the garden.

I am on the road. The dandelions on the bank have flowered, and are waiting for the wind before they can make their parachute landings. Further down, by the bog, they are still flowering. Dandelions know their time wonderfully well. Perhaps they will inherit the earth. After us, and before the forest.

I come to a bend in the road. There is a big birch tree around whose roots the earth is so parched that only thin grass and a couple of tiny pine trees grow there, and juniper, which roe – elk – hares attack in winter.

*

Across the corner of the meadow, I reach a cluster of birches.

A blackcock starts into flight. I look back. A rooftop. The end of the woodshed. The flowers of the common lilac ending, the Hungarian lilac coming into bloom.

Further away, beside the other road, Ott and Lemmit are playing badminton.

Two swallows whirl above the meadow. Perhaps the same ones who have just begun to make a nest in the byre and pecked clay from the pond Lauris has dug in the garden.

Beside the house, by the lilacs, stands an aerial, now turned toward the south. For the last half hour it has been showing Italian TV. Under the picture, in the right-hand corner, a little RAI. There was a film on. A woman died, a man escaped, running along the road, until he collapsed.

*

The forest receives me – that, at least, can be said. Ground elder, hazelwort, hazel trees reaching up desperately toward the tops of the birches, which flee before them.

A puddle swarming with mosquitoes. The earth dappled with flowering millet grass. Coppiced woodland. A young coppice on an old meadow.

Raspberry canes, ferns, around large stones which were once rolled here from the meadow.

Spruce scrub, which grows with certainty, as if knowing it will have the last laugh, that it has come to stay.

Beside my foot, yellow archangel. *Galeobdolon.* The ground layer. The lower world, the underworld.

Who lives in this underworld? I push aside the wood horsetail and the yellow archangel. Last year's leaves, as yet unrotted. Little heaps of twigs, among which someone creeps, climbs, *lives*.

Under them the greyish earth, the end result and the beginning of life.

And on all sides the mosquitoes, the *mosquitoes*, which do not allow you to commune with this life.

In the upper air, someone is singing. Perhaps a robin – *Erithacus*. And now it flies down to an alder branch, flirts its tail and looks at me.

But the mosquitoes are winning. The mosquitoes have won. I go on.

*

I duck beneath a fallen birch tree. The leaves are still green, but much of the bark is loose: it has fallen between two nearby alders.

As I write this, I can smell the scent of the alder and the birch.

Somewhere, a blackbird is singing. Its song harmonizes so well with the gloomy air.

A line from Eliot, I think: 'And wood thrush singing through the fog o my daughter . . .'

Strawberries, strawberries in flower. A maple, lost in the forest. The ground begins to rise.

Here the wood horsetail holds sway. The woodrush has already flowered. The mosquitoes have found my traces in the air, and therefore also me. The mosquitoes dictate the form of my writing.

The edge of the meadow. Heartsease. A single heartsease in flower.

A couple of birch-stumps. Our language does not have a proper word for them, or we have forgotten it. I recall that in the Ostyak language there is a word that means a standing, dried-up birch-stump. Marsh titmice still sometimes make their nests in such birch-stumps. But in this stump only tinder fungus makes its home. A single butterfly larva has frozen still on the moss.

A few blue and yellow blades of cow-wheat have come out of the shelter of the forest and into the meadow — where they are like strangers from another world.

And here are the speedwells. A carpet of blue speedwells. Like eyes. Like a glimpse into the distance. A glimpse full of distance or sky: what else is the sky but distance.

*

I am on a gritted road. It was rolled smooth once. But badly; stones emerged, and now the road is full of pebbles.

By the roadside willowherb, brushwood, rowan, alder. As if the forest were drawing curtains around itself to prevent strangers seeing in.

Sometimes the curtain tears: crack willow stretched out along the ground and in the interior of the forest — the chaotic colonnade of spruce-stumps — is open to the gaze.

Here the bank by the roadside is full of rough horsetail. Just like lattices — prison bars.

I want to explore this road more quickly. I do not want to meet anyone. In the countryside, in the forest, meeting another person is too overwhelming an experience, like an axe-blow that cuts the threads of thought and imagination, frightening you, so that you tumble out of the ivory tower of your poetic solitude, look at the oncomer, say 'Hello', but no sound emerges from your parched throat, so you say something, answer a few questions, but feel that you are doing it as though from a great distance, through thick glass or water. No, it is not good to meet anyone on this road. I am now, finally, an escapee. I need solitude. The forest. For solitude is like the forest or the sea. Solitude is space, open space.

*

Where, then, is the beginning of the path? The forest has already covered it, enveloped it with lace curtains. Cow parsley. Raspberry canes. Nettles.

But finally I find it, all the same. I step through a clump of nettles. I am in the forest. No, as Wiedemann's German dictionary might say, the forest and women's arses belong to everyone. Not so. Each can look after itself. When necessary.

What would I do if someone were suddenly to come and see me writing and ask what I am doing. Would I say that I was writing poetry? Hardly. It is so embarrassing – writing poetry. Since my childhood, I have always written poetry in secret. And tried to write poetry as if I was not really writing poetry. Prose is a more serious matter, a prose-writer is a more serious and businesslike kind of person, he has more right to look other people in the eye. But even he does not really work, like a chauffeur or a painter or a printer or a plumber. Among the mass of humanity you are always rather suspect. It is different in the forest. The forest does not care who you are outside; here you are, in some way, one of us or a stranger. It is good in the forest.

In fact, I want to do something – something I do not know myself and others do not know, either, that I do it.

I pull my hood over my head. On the right-hand side, by the path, is a crooked, mossy, thick-stemmed birch. Already long familiar to me.

Beside the birch, an ash. Young and straight. There are few ashes in this forest; most of them are close to the farmsteads, where the wind carries seeds from garden ash trees.

The path itself is already clearer, the nettles and plantains are behind me. Beneath my feet are fallen leaves, sparse short grass, thorns and heaps of twigs. I am in the real forest. Here I can no longer be seen from the road. Here I can be alone. Can be myself, or someone else – it is all the same, here it does not make much difference.

I would like to think a little. To find associations, metaphors. But the mosquitoes will not allow it. The mosquitoes keep you mercilessly in contact with the direct reality which, as a philosopher, you are unable to capture, which is usually called the present.

No wonder, then, that our people did not produce speculative philosophers. We had mosquitoes.

*

By the path, a diminutive oak with leaves a span long. Then five fir trees, their trunks grown together.

I'm really writing a travel book. This time I could not go to Sweden; so I have come to this forest.

One path turns aside. To where, a little further off, there is in the midst of the forest the site of a cellar, and a couple of half-parched bullaces – all that is left of a farmstead.

Where the path now is was once perhaps something more – a road between farmsteads.

Roads, too, have their own history and destiny. Some narrow, half-overgrown forest paths may once have been real roads leading to the mill, the manor or the post road. Some paths have perhaps never been big, but are very old – hundreds and hundreds of years: they connected the first farmsteads.

But before people there were animals, and the paths of animals, along which it was easier to go than through the brushwood. In some places, animal paths became human paths, but the history of the animal path was lost in obscurity – it could be thousands of years old. Even ant paths can remain the same for decades, even more than a century.

The roads and paths of the age of the horse were modest: a farm cart did not need a wide, gritted road through this forest. Now, in the age of the tractor, roads are altogether more conspicuous – like gashes in the forest's skin. They are marked by deep ruts, crushed saplings, lesions in the trunks of the roadside trees.

Here someone has cleared a road, felled and cast aside a couple of alders whom the winter snow had weighed down across the road. The alders rot where they fell.

The dandelion does not yet blossom here. In the open, its brothers and sisters have already flowered. Brothers and sisters! For it is hermaphroditic, at once man and woman.

If only we, too, were hermaphroditic. We could let the gametes live their own lives, we would not be the slaves of our own sex cells!

*

The road goes downward. Ahead, in the middle of the road, is a rotten pile of brushwood on which thick moss has already grown. Someone has stepped on it.

The road continues downward. A blossoming dandelion marks the beginning of the marsh. The road disappears. I turn right, onto another road.

*

A path on a bank by the edge of the marsh. On the ground, only aspen leaves and needles and twigs. Here and there some wood sorrel. On the forest floor, bilberry bushes.

A spider climbs up the half-written page. Like a character from some other alphabet. Perhaps it is?!

On the ground, in all directions, young pines, which have not been able to rival the birches or alders for growth. They grew themselves to death, without reaching the light.

It is as if I had written it with my own blood. The mosquitoes took the tribute.

Suddenly I see, by the side of the path, skulls and jawbones. A fox? A raccoon dog? A badger? Unfortunately I do not recognize the bones, although I ought to know them.

This path, too, ends in the middle of the forest, among lilies of the valley.

Somewhere above, rain falls.

*

I am high up on a ridge. A large juniper grows here. To see the crown, I have to crane my neck. The crown is still green.

It is time to turn back. I go a little to one side. Close to where the skull lies, I find someone's burrow, before the mouth of the burrow some scooped-out sand.

But there are no signs of life. No animal tracks, only the marks of the rain in the sand.

Perhaps it was, in fact, a badger path I came along? But they say that raccoon dogs have driven out the badgers. In our district, too?

This page is getting wet. I creep under a tree, here I can write. The mosquitoes no longer rise high, but swarm around the skull like a grey cloud.

A wood warbler is singing. The rain made the grass on the path wet, and then stopped.

Something is falling from above. Raindrops? Pine cones?

I am back on my own tracks. Broken stalks, flattened grass.

It was real rain. There are large raindrops on the leaves of the undergrowth.

*

Back on the road. A real forest road under the ancient trees. A couple of pine trees have fallen across it. So now, it is no longer travelled. But it was once travelled: the ruts of cartwheels and perhaps tractor wheels can still be made out.

On the left-hand side is primeval forest, on the right, on a bank, young pines and birches. A former field which, in the collective farm period, became brushwood, and the brushwood forest.

I walk along the ridge. Below, in the valley, grow birches. I am level with their crowns.

The rain falls on the letter c.

Great stumps crisscrossed by the roadside and on the road.

Violets – bright flowers with no scent. I take a couple and put them in my notebook.

The soles of my feet are wet, I slip on pine cones. I look up: a parched, forked pine. Someone's hoarse cry of warning.

The sun came out for a moment. Shadows appeared on the page.

The warning cry also comes from somewhere high above. There is something a little like a breaking twig, but it is not that.

Creak – creak, creak – creak.

A small oak, under it a handful of last year's bleached leaves – just the same colour as the skull.

*

A ride, toward the sun, which is behind cloud once more.

Along the ride, the undulation of the landscape is clearly visible. The hillier land remained forest, the flatter became fields.

A steep inclination. It is as if the road is cut by the bank. I look down into the valley. Dark stumps with a covering of wood sorrel. Everything is so peaceful. A robin is singing.

By the roadside are fir cones. Extraordinary: I had not noticed them before.

The mosquitoes: do they fly with me all the time, or do they swop about between themselves? How far can a single mosquito fly? One should mark them and examine the matter.

A clump of pine trees. The grey, timeless forest floor. Just thorns, pine cones, branches, a couple of recumbent tree trunks that the forest is gradually burying beneath litter and moss.

Somewhere here lay a body which old Maali saw sometime in the 1950s somewhere in the forest, as he said. He went to the forest to pick berries and suddenly saw a dead woman, was badly frightened, ran home and said nothing to anyone.

The vegetation becomes more luxuriant. The road disappears a couple of times. Under the trees is a lot of honeysuckle – it is flowering.

Pigs have been rootling there: there are snout- and hoofmarks to be seen.

I take a short-cut through the bushes and soon arrive back at the pigs' grubbing ground.

A few years ago I saw, here, a nestful of black grouse chicks. The mother fled before me, feigning injury, the chicks scattered into the undergrowth. I did not allow the black grouse mother to lead me astray; I crouched down on the ground and looked

for the chicks. I found a couple of them under some tussocks;
when I stretched out my hand to grab hold of them, they fled,
helping themselves with their stumpy wings. One ran across
the palm of my hand – soft, dappled and unbelievably light,
like a child's breath. Its lightness was so marvellous that I still
remember it.

They, too, fled – from you, a human being. Just as you yourself
flee. From people, from yourself.

Now a thrush chick struggles into flight from your path.
Its wings carry it, but its tail is still short. It tries to land on
a branch, but it does not succeed, it falls into the grass and
is lost from view.

One more short-cut. On each side, proud honeysuckle
and sweet white currants. Between the bushes nettles and
ground elder.

Tractor-wheel ruts. A pine that has fallen across the road
has been cut into pieces and taken away, only the crown
remains, between the tightly packed trees.

*

A cuckoo is singing.

The sun comes out.

Suddenly I am in a clearing. Cow parsley and herb bennet
grow here. The scent of sun and summer, which is impossible to
define. The scent is the most anonymous thing generally. We can
say where it comes from and where it goes, but not what it is.

Amid the brushwood and the nettles are a couple of upright
charred timbers and haystack poles, also charred.

I go there: in the shade of the nettles are the remains of a roof,
half-burned wall planks. Here was once a hay barn. The clearing
used to be a hay field. Once we took shelter in the hay barn
from the rain. We drew on the walls with coal – I drew Chinese
characters, Malle Estonian ornaments, and the children cars.

Where did we get the coal? Yes, there was a fireplace. Fires
had been lit there. No more.

A crow calls out its name a couple of times and whirls toward the clearing.

Moss has already started to grow on the charred timbers.

*

There has been digging here. The bank has been thrown up into a mound so that the bare shingle shows. Two or three openings where young trees are already growing.

Gravel pits? Wartime gun emplacements?

The road leads to the marsh. A couple more wood anemones, which elsewhere have already flowered. A marsh marigold.

Elk tracks in the boggy ground, which is already squelching underfoot.

Liverwort on the tussocks. Ditches on either side of the road. In the middle of the road a drying puddle, the ground around it covered in duckweed – yes, this puddle has already been here for a long time.

Between the tussocks, I catch sight of twayblades – orchids, which have always pleased me with their greenish flowers and large, veined leaves.

Here, the tractor-man has felled young birches and alders and thrown them crisscross over the road so that the marshy surface will carry better.

A murmuring begins to sound. A rivulet. Perhaps the beginning of a river. A sodden log for crossing it; on the log, a dung-heap. Otter? Mink?

Right in the middle of the flowing water is a tussock; on the tussock a meadow rue flowers.

There is no rubbish to be seen. In the peaty deeps a couple of caddis fly climb; on the water's surface glide magpie moths.

Barbed wire has been drawn across the stream and along the side of the road. There was once a cattle run here.

Overgrown with wood stitchwort, the road leads up to the bank once more.

Hazelwort. A solitary dandelion. You linger to ponder how a dandelion seed floated here from somewhere on the edge of field or garden.

Buckthorn. One large one and two small ones. They are flowering at this moment.

A couple of sturdy aspens. A forked birch, fallen on its side. It has lived its life, now tinder fungus is living off it, in clusters.

*

Another clearing and hay barn – this time whole.

The former hay field, now long unmown. Thick foggage, chest-high cow parsley. The forest begins its conquest from the edge, the alders first – they grow from suckers. It is harder for the others – the seedlings cannot push through the tall grass.

Beside the hay barn lies a pile of freshly painted planks, scented in the sunlight. In the hay barn, on armfuls of hay, lie lumps of salt, which the animals must have licked in winter.

Among the hay two jars, one empty, in the other a little fatty meat. The jars have an air of secrecy. They recall the Forest Brethren, poachers. You look around: suddenly someone is following you, his finger on the trigger . . .

The planks must cover some opening – was there a cellar there?

But of course. On this spot a solitary apple tree still blossoms, and a great, lofty linden tree. Only stumps are left of the plum and cherry trees. The site of the house itself is covered in raspberry canes.

Beside the linden tree is an old birch. The lowest branches of the linden have sunk to the ground. Some of them will, in time, become a new tree.

*

A high hill with solitary pine trees. Dry, sparsely grassed, smelling of resin. A small piece of a purer, brighter world here in this wearisome, humid exuberance.

The road begins again on the other side of the clearing.

A rotten gate has been cast to one side. Barbed wire on the ground. Otherwise you would not even notice you were stepping across a border which for some people was as strict and real as the strip of land and barbed wire on the beach at Sõrve or near Toolse.

Here heifers were grazed. It has been said that some escaped from the area surrounded by barbed wire, lived free in the forest and ran wild. They could no longer be caught, and in the end huntsmen shot them dead like forest creatures.

The barbed wire has grown into the tree trunks. The trees do not recover from it, the wound stays forever.

The barbed wire grows into the trees, *not allowed*, *forbidden* into the consciousness.

Barbed wire, it is said, is necessary, absolute freedom does not exist.

But who was it that thought up absolute freedom? Who has, at any time, demanded or wanted it?

For one should not say that it is good that there is pain, when barbed wire grows into tree trunks and consciousnesses.

The birch weeps sap, the spruce resin, the alder blood, we make poetry.

Barbed wire rusts, the gate rots.

The road runs through and over the pain. The pain is a signal.

*

Another clearing. More dandelions. The road runs along the barbed wire. So do I. I do not know whether I am going in the right direction.

The docks on the path take a deep breath before flowering, before they begin to grow their tall stems.

Now I go through the marsh. Bulrushes grow here – there must be underground water close by. There are bootmarks on the boggy road. This does not please me. I want to tread roads that I have not trodden and where human feet do not often tread.

Dandelions in a hay field – the flowers yellow, the seed heads white.

The excited chatter of fieldfares in the alder thicket. The dandelion. The red-leaved ground elder.

I peel the young shoot of some hedge mustard and eat it. It tastes good. The young stems of the warted bunias are also good. It was my grandfather who taught me to eat hedge mustard. I learned about the warted bunias from some botanists when I was on a field trip with them in northeast Estonia.

By the roadside, a wild apple tree: someone once threw an apple-core away here. Just as in the forest near our house, where five little apple trees grow close together – for an apple does indeed have five seed-chambers.

At the foot of a spruce tree stands an ants' nest. The ants' path leads upward along the trunk – they go there to cultivate aphids.

On the ground, a box of Djubek cigarettes – a letter yet to be read.

The forest must erase our writing. Even that which we once wrote on the wall of the now burned hay barn.

The forest does not accept us except through death, or something that is the same as death. Becoming another, abandoning signs . . .

One road more. It still cannot be the right one: the forest tricks us. It wants to erase everything we have left in it, all culture, to replace it with nature, which lives in a different time, which has a completely different kind of memory.

It is only a logging path, with a couple of blocks of wood lying on it, which have escaped the attention of the loggers.

Here an elk has torn the bark from a spruce tree. On the one hand an elk, on the other, barbed wire. Far above, a finch sings.

*

Look! The forest did not hide the roads completely, after all. The path winds through raspberry canes and brushwood. Another few dozen steps and I reach a hillock, the spruce trees that have been planted there.

Once this must have been a field, a strawberry slope. What a good influence the collective farm system had on the birches, the alders, the dandelions and the strawberries – the first to occupy the uncultivated land.

A female roe starts up and flees with a rustle into the alder brushwood.

Insects with long antennae (I am not sure whether they are some kind of bee or fly) circle above the slope, very close to the ground. Is their nest here (in which case they must be bees), or are they looking for something to eat?

There is a moment to see what is and grows here. Milkwort. Mellick, which is now stretching out its flowers. Vetch.

The wood warbler tinkles on this spot: silk–solk, silk–solk.

I try to find a way through. It is quieter and more peaceful than before. the wind is quieter, perhaps the forest offers better shelter. The sky is growing clouds again.

There is limestone gravel on the slope. How did it get there?

I climb up to some alders, which are lying on the former road. A clear felling has been made here; the spruces remain, everything else has been felled to the ground.

*

I would like to fly. There are no thickets in the air. And you cannot leave tracks in the air. I am tired of this luxuriance, this ground elder, these nettles, these raspberries!

To sandy ground, to stony ground. To moorland. Scrubland – Saaremaa, Muhu.

Here is a small river. In the water is a series of stones, so that one can cross it. On the other side, on a hillock, are a strawberry wood, sparse spruce trees and a cluster of birches.

On the forest floor, beside the path, a solitary columbine, one flower already open.

*

The forest opens up, and the first thing I see is a purple lilac.

The marsh stretches right up to the farmyard. There is a belt of sedge clumps. I go through a thicket of meadowsweet; the dry stems of last year's plants snap under my feet.

A white lilac protects the foundations of the house. The hay shed, where a fieldfare once made its nest, has collapsed; a few rotten splinters of planks are all that is left of the beehives.

The cowhouse and the threshing room have also collapsed. The frame of an old buckboard crouches on the caved-in roof as if it had fallen down from the sky.

By the wall lies a decaying cartwheel. The front door has been lifted off its hinges and placed over the well. How many small animals have drowned in that well?

Beside the steps is an overturned cauldron, full of holes; on the steps dandelions, cow parsley and nettles grow luxuriantly.

Inside the house is a poetic, surrealist confusion. The windows have been broken – a year ago they were still whole – and lie on the floor, along with rags, pieces of sewing patterns, rotting screws and clothes pegs.

Here is still a crooked file with a handle, a chocolate-box lid, a piece of a felt boot and a couple of small bottles.

Underpants, curtains, a cow hook – this farmstead, too, stood in pasture-land, and the heifers pushed their way into the house to shelter from the rain. It is said that one once fell into the cellar.

Broken, rusted tongs. The back of a wireless. A loom-end. A rusty sieve. A couple of oil lamps without glasses. A shoe. Two cans of food.

A plywood valise and a horse's saddle have disintegrated on the range.

In the corner of the kitchen is a larder. Here stand a small milk pail, a group of bottles and boots and shoes. I put a couple of the more interesting chemist's bottles and a one-third litre bottle in my pocket, and also take a glass decanter stopper – perhaps it will fit the carafe without a cork at home.

In the drying room are a couple of barrels. The kiln is still standing. In the middle of the earth floor is a cellar whose ceiling has fallen in – other junk has also fallen into the cellar.

The potato cellar (which the heifer fell into) is under the room. A trap door through the foundations leads to it.

It is no longer easy to get under the drying barn – but the flour chest, a motorcycle frame, a broken pitchfork and a scythe are still there.

To the attic room I do not go. There, once, were double windows, a store of beehives and a chest with balls of rag strips and honeycomb frames.

A family of bees once came to the chest – probably they were attracted by the smell of the honeycombs. I came here at night – it was around midsummer, and the night was light – I drove the bees into a swarming box and brought them home. I came a different, shorter way than this time. I also brought the chest home – I drilled the wooden nails out, broke the chest down into planks, stuffed them lengthways into a large rucksack, took them away and reassembled them in an outbuilding at home.

Someone had thrown the balls of rag strips through the attic window, surely the same person who had smashed the panes of the double windows. I think that there was more than one of them – a solitary person does not generally do such damage.

The garden linden tree has already stretched out its branches almost as far as the steps and against the roof. It has many flower buds.

A redwing singing in the top of the linden tree flies to a spruce on the other side of the house and goes on singing there.

It must be time to go.

I go inside the house once more and take the valise with me. Inside the valise are a couple of butterflies' wings. Again these daylight emperor moths: they creep inside to take shelter from the winter and become booty for the mice, who eat away the sleeping body and leave the wings behind.

From beyond the forest, the wind brings children's voices. From the other side echoes the distant rumble of a tractor.

In the garden there is still a half-dried-out cherry tree. Most of the flowers have flowered, and it looks as if there will also be some berries.

At the edge of the garden dandelions and columbines gather.

The first alders have already reached the first plum trees.

I start back along my own tracks. Some overturned leaves. Ground elder.

The sedge tussocks are crushed in places. Where I used them to jump over the watery places.

There are many things the forest has to mend.

*

On the ground is something white – no, it is not paper, it is birch bark.

I think: poetry is like walking somewhere. A poem, then, is a wandering. But you take the actual walk within yourself. If you do. You set off as one, you come back as another. If you do.

I have spent half a day walking among the green. But I do not see the green, I am colour-blind. The green which I see is not green. If it were green, I would perhaps have more peace.

Does my consciousness know what is green? Does it recognize green? I suppose I shall never know.

Perhaps, indeed, my longing is a longing for a green which I cannot see, but which I should remember, which should be in my genes?

Common lady's mantle. *Alchemilla.* Alchemical water among the lady's mantles. Flowers which are officially rosaceous, but to the untrained eye are difficult even to distinguish.

A birch gall. By the roots, an armful of gnarled wood, as if it had for the time being forgotten where to grow and, so, grown far in every direction.

*

I turn to one side, into the sparser forest. Here are bilberry stems, while under the spruce trees the ground is full of May lilies.

On a hillock stands a spruce split by lightning. Splinters ten metres long, as if cut by an axe.

I take one with me; it is light and arched, like a water drain.

I go toward a little marsh – bilberries, sphagnum moss farther off. Somehow tranquil. Another couple of drops of rain.

Actually, I have gone farther from myself. I have paid so little attention to myself, I have lived only outward, toward the forest, the bilberries and the pines. Now I am going home, and toward myself. Now I notice that my feet are wet and tired, my back sweaty, my face and neck bitten by mosquitoes.

What are they doing at home? Is Italian TV still showing? Are they already eating? Have they been shopping?

The roebuck has scraped a patch on the road. The sand is showing – grey, clean sand. How is it able to grow those mighty spruces and pines?

The strength of the earth has indeed gone into the trees. As a mother's health and strength goes into her children.

Once again, the place where the house used to stand. The maple, lilac, and around the maple the ground is full of little maples.

The marsh. Somewhere a trench or drain is blocked, and the water does not run away. A group of parched maples and between them, by the pool, bog arum grows luxuriantly.

Two spruces are here, outstretched, their roots free of the ground; the hole left in the earth is already a black, watery bog. The marsh mounts its attack.

The edge of the forest. A pile of large stones, by them field scabious and, farther off, bracken.

Here is the road. The sun is shining again.

A whinchat is singing on the telephone line, farther off, in the bushes, a reed warbler.

In the pond a lake frog is croaking, the green frog that lives in water.

I walk across the meadow. The grass is no longer particularly wet. The mosquitoes stay close to the ground.

A skylark is singing high above.

The old road is overgrown, it hardly exists any longer. A hay truck has made a new road beside it.

I reach the hill. In front of me I see the white willows and spruces. Then the slate roof.

Here is home. Here I live. Here we live.

DUST. I MYSELF

I

I, too, was born of the longing of dust.
Dust wants to live.
Dust wants to dance, sing, dust wants eyes, a mouth, backbone
    and intestines, dust wants to speak of its longing for life
    and light,
of how it is weary of being dust.
Dust speaks and whimpers even as dust, but its words and
    voice, too, are merely dust,
so that it is difficult for us to say which is which.
Which is dust, which voice, which yearning,
which am I, which are we.

Am I a speck of dust or its voice, another speck of dust?
A speck of dust, or its longing to be something else?
Am I silence or voice, dust's silence or its voice,
which contains everything from Gilgamesh to the sorrows of
    young Werther?
From Gilgamesh, who wanted to know Earth's law,
although he who comes to know Earth's law is left weeping
    on the ground.
Enkidu, who was already dust once more, spoke to him:
'Did you see him whom the mast killed?' 'I saw him,
he is under the earth and is dragging forth posts.'
'Did you see him who died . . . ?' 'I saw him,
he sleeps in the bed of night and drinks fresh water.'
'Did you see him who was killed in battle?' 'I saw him;
his father and mother comfort him
and his wife bends over him.'
'Did you see him whose body was thrown on to the
    wasteland?' 'I saw him;
his soul beneath the Earth does not rest in peace.'
'Did you see him whose soul is not honoured?' 'I saw him;
he eats scrapings from the pot and crumbs of bread
which have been thrown into the street.'

But you, spermatozoon, semen.

You, too, received your longing from somewhere, your longing
    for the warm, dark primal fluid

in which your, my, our ancestors, once swam, divided, and
    united again.

The sea. *Thalassa. Thalatta.*

The sea, of which so little now remains.

Sometimes it is memory, sometimes our own blood.

Sometimes sea water, which in Norway during the war was used
for blood transfusions, when there was not enough blood.

Sometimes it is a warm, salty source in a woman's, *your* body, in
    which once again the miracle of union recurs.

You sense something, like a thread, a cord along which
    Cambrian, Jurassic, Tertiary, earlier centuries send their
    messages to future times which do not yet have names,

to countries, kingdoms which do not yet have names.

To peoples who speak languages which do not yet have names.

You are on your way there, sperm, chromosomes, tiny egoistical
    genes.

I believe that you are a message – then I am the commentary
    of that message, its translation into flesh and blood – take,
    eat – only I do not know what it means.

If anything at all.

But does the fact that it means anything or nothing itself mean
    anything?

Let us think of the sea. And that there is something greater than
    all questions.

Something that reaches over all borders.

Water, foam, stones, sand.

Wind.

Sometimes warm, sometimes cold.

3

We do not often think that we, too, are written
and that in that which we write there is actually less of ourselves
    than of others.
Ancestors, genes, heard, seen and read.
We are variations on a theme which first resounded in some
    primal fluid, the theme *life, life.*
It would be easy to believe that in us this theme is heard most
    clearly, most perfectly and most beautifully.
But it is hard for me to believe it.
Too much have I watched birds, identified plants and planted
    trees and read in nature books strange tales of insects, spiders,
    cephalopods and birds.
I recall the bowerbird, which builds a cabin for its wedding
    festivities and dyes it with berry-juices.
I recall the spider, which places a spot of glue on the end of a
    thread and uses it, like the gaucho his bola, to catch its prey.
I recall the termite and the ant, which in their hollow, subterranean
    nests grow mushrooms for their nourishment.
I recall something of the language of the dolphin and the bee,
    the beaver's dam-building, the elephant which touches the
    skull of a dead elephant with its trunk.
And many, many others, and when I think also of what we
    have done to all of them,
when I think of safaris, whale hunters, birds dying of oil pollution
    and poisoned rivers
it is difficult, almost impossible for me to believe that we are the
    most beautiful voice in the world's music.
Yes, perhaps the *Kalevala*, perhaps the song of Gilgamesh,
perhaps Mozart, perhaps Norbert Wiener,
perhaps gloves from Muhu or the song of the Chukchi.
But there are so few of them, there are in the world impossibly
    few people
who are able to make anything really beautiful, and there are
    ever fewer of them.
I fear that most of us are a badly played tune, a rattling, a rumbling,
    noise which is gradually extinguishing the great music of life.

We are a part of life that smashes the whole, teeth that gnaw the
    breast, a hand that breaks the fingers of another hand.
For teeth cannot bite themselves, fingers cannot break themselves.
One can destroy oneself only when there is still something.
The universe cannot destroy itself.
An accidental phrase, an accidental comfort.

4

But then: is the noise merely a noise, or does it conceal something
    more?
Do we not play (or is there not played on us) a completely
    different music, cosmic and divine?
For dust has its own dust, and dust's dust its own: in moving from
    great to small we meet, in turn, order and chaos, and finally
    arrive at atoms and even smaller particles, in which all is once
    again, in its own way, regular.
Perhaps the music of the spheres lives yet in the music of the
    electrons and elementary particles – for it exists also in us,
    in our bodies.
But we do not have much in common with our atoms – we live
    on the outer surfaces of our bodies, without reaching the
    depths, we are like slicks of oil on the water's surface.
And the atoms within us are unconscious that we are we (if we
    are!), that they are part of a person, a knife, a daffodil or a
    stone in a field.
    But in their world there is no life or death, either; they do not
notice how inanimate material becomes animate, or vice versa.
    We live so much higher than ourselves, we live above our
own heads.
    We are like wind and clouds, like a folk tale or like the gods
in heaven.
    We may live by the light of our own words and myths, in our
own philosophies and castles in the air.

Until they come to fetch us and we fall down into this dusty middle world. (Perhaps there is no dust in heaven, and that makes heaven heaven.)

And we do not understand, either here or there, whether we are noise or music, and if music, then what kind of music.

Or what folk tale, what dream, what existence – questions that do not receive an answer even as we fall for the last time, as our own dust mixes with other dust, but *we ourselves? We ourselves?*

To fight for the rights and freedoms of the body,
for arms and legs, mouths and eyes, lungs and livers,
for brains, inner ears and outer ears,
for sex glands and sweat glands, nails and hair,
whom we mercilessly exploit,
whom we force to work for our own good, day and night,
whom we do not allow to live their own lives,
choose their partners or beget offspring according to their
     own wishes.
We subordinate the limbs to the brain and force the brain,
instead of interesting thoughts, to think about food and sex,
to imagine stupid fancies, to dwell on our
feelings of inferiority, hypochondria and jealousy
and to govern the other parts of the body. Even in sleep
it is not free of our worries or complexes.
And like a Viking prince, who was buried with
his horses, his women and his servants,
we force our own enslaved parts of the body
to die with us. Only our nails and hair
can, for a few days, grow freely, but they, too,
hardly know what to do
with this sudden and brief freedom.

But it does come. *Eppur si viene.*
Comes, when I have closed my eyes.
Comes and looks at my open notebook,
smiles and shakes the apple trees
so that the black cats fall
and get mixed up with the white cats,
the yellow chrysanthemums with the loudspeakers
and I slip downwards
as once on the lakeshore on the Karelian isthmus
down the granite slope from the white night
straight into the dark lake water.

All that I have written
is so different.
All that I have written
is so similar.
That similarity is nothing certain, no foundation,
rather that which changes, a wind, which blows
through the foundations. A wind.

It is foolish to think that an object is one thing
and its movement something else.
Existence cannot be divided into arrows and flight,
particles and their trajectories.
Arrow and flight are one. For the particle is
its own trajectory. I am my life.
I live my life. Life lives me.
Life and living are one.
Also when there is no 'me'.
Not yet. At this moment. Any more.

I, too, know something about the bridge of Cinvat.
Simply, that I have been somewhere near it
and I believe that before me the bridge lies not along,
but across. Man is a sort of sleep,
Gurdjieff once said. Once you step over
the knife-edge, there is no longer any good or evil.
That does not mean that on the other side
you can sleep with all the women and take
another man's house and dash the heads of his children
against a stone. There
sleep is really sleep and wakefulness wakefulness.
And it does not matter what is said
about this side. This side is like
the model of Halmahera island which I saw in a dream:
a small conservatory, where had been brought a few palms,
flowers and butterflies. But I knew
that it was only a model, that the real island
was far away and unreachable. It does not matter
how far you are on the other side, there is always something
even further. There is a more heavenly heaven
and a more hellish hell. I suppose for some
we are hell, and for some heaven.
Oh heaven, how tedious it all is,
like an endless monotonous jogging
up and down stairs. But outside
it is already evening. The sky is bright.
And the stars are shining. The stars are shining.

At night it freezes, there are no tracks.
By day it thaws, by day there are tracks
on the road and by the roadside; the tracks stay
until, at evening, it freezes again, until the earth freezes
with all its tracks. Night comes.
No tracks are left at night, night comes without leaving tracks.
But today's tracks will perhaps remain until
the great thaw, perhaps until spring.
The tracks of our shoes and rubber boots
on the muddy gravel road under the ice and snow.
But night comes and goes without leaving tracks.
Night comes and goes.
Comes and goes.

This autumn's great big yellow chrysanthemum,
it does not flower; it is Flowering itself,
which in it receives the form of a flower, which is a flower.
Just as the girl whom we meet on Vanemuine hill
is Meeting in the form of the girl,
just as the moon is Shining as moon
and I myself am
Coming Home from School with Child
as Jaan and Lemmit. Only I do not know
what/who expresses itself in language, in this language
which has two heads. If you turn it round,
it begins to spawn Ideas and Gods,
splits us and our everyday affairs
into a playground for the heavenly host,
shadows on the cave wall, which for some reason believe
that the subject must be more real than the predicate
or the other way round. Although I have known
what is real: the stones which the boys threw
at the old saucepan in the yard. And the grapevines
around the veranda. Sometimes the spring sky. Sometimes
    dreams.

I read a couple of poems by Paal-Helge Haugen
and then thought of the sea, the distant sea, vanishing into
    drizzle
at Bygdøy, near Oslo. I did not see
the open sea that time, the ocean of tide and ebb,
the vastness that neither sight nor imagination grasps:
for we cannot see infinity, we only seek the limit,
and marvel when we cannot find it. From that marvelling
much is born, including, in its way,
what is written here. But then
I happened to read, in Plotinus,
'. . . but the infinite is terrible and belongs to an opposing
    order'
(an order other than that of beauty, goodness and the finite).
    Then I understood more clearly
that my soul is not at home in the Mediterranean lands
where all is so definite, clear and final. In me
is something that belongs so well
with low clouds, fog over the Atlantic
or the blue spring haze of Tai shan
and a mist into which there disappears a man with a grey
    beard,
wearing an old cape, under his arm a roll of paper, although
    I know
that I shall never know who he is, or whether he exists.
I, too, belong to an opposing order.

Birch tops like brushes
paint the dark darker, the light lighter;
paint dark on darkness,
light on light.
The light remains the thinner:
the tattered shirt of the tattered year.
The gleam of bare skin – it is neither
darkness nor light,
this nor that.
I do not know what it is.
I do not know what I know and do not know.
I do not even know what the sparse
black brushes of the birch branches
write, paint on the dark clouds,
of themselves, of their present,
which has gone, which exists
no longer even as I see it,
when the light from between those branches
has reached my eyes and mind.
For we see only a lost world,
only what is no longer.

Her head shorn, the maiden enters the wall.
Two swallows fly in and are caught in the wall.
Papyruses and lilies grow in through the window and are
    caught in the wall.
A monkey with a lyre comes from the hill and steps onto the
    wall.
Then the earth trembles and the people flee;
the hill awakens and buries the houses beneath ash and stones;
but this they no longer see, do not see, or
how, one after another, come the winter rains
and on the site of the town grass grows green and crocuses
    sprout,
and daffodils and hyacinths, how people and swallows
gradually return, how everything is forgotten,
the sun rises and sets more than a million times,
but they are still there. Venetians and Turks
come and go, but they know nothing about it.
We come and go, dig them out from between the walls,
photograph them and draw them, write books about them
but they know nothing about it. What they are
is no more than a single mark, a mark that means
only spring, a mark that means that spring
is itself everlasting, the same as love.

You wait for a taxi. Time trickles through you like grey sand.
You are like a funnel, like an old hourglass,
which actually flows like sand, like time itself,
only more slowly, through you. You yourself crumble
like a riverbank, gradually join the flow,
ever faster. Through the hourglass. Through the flowing.
Through the cars and the waiting-for-cars. Soot falls on snow,
but there is no warmth. It comes to nothing, nothingness.
A dark nowhere into which flow sand and hourglasses.
The holiday visitors stub out their cigarettes in the sand,
spread their towels over birds' nests and fledglings.
But then comes someone who spreads a towel over them,
their wives, mothers, mothers-in-law and sons.
There is no explosion, there is no ending. We do not burn,
we suffocate. The taxi arrives. There is no more time.
There is no more space. There is no more land.
There is no more air. There is no more water.
There is no more fire. There are no more roads or truth.
There is a taxi. A free taxi.

There is still an hour left of this year. I would still like to write something. The electric clock ticks noiselessly: between the hour and the minute a little colon pulses – seconds.

I write a word about every two seconds. Sometimes I must also think, so time is short. Perhaps I will have time to fill this sheet of paper.

Five minutes have passed. There are still fifty-five minutes of this year. Five just became six. So, fifty-four. According to Moscow time. Eastern European time would give us an hour's grace. On Eastern European time, we would be younger.

While I have been sitting here, the children have eaten some ginger biscuits and an apple, many people in the world have died, and still more have been born.

A couple of pieces of coal have burned to ash and a couple of specks of dust have fallen on this piece of paper. Here they are are not visible; on the black radio, they are.

On the table is an open book. In it is an article about Ugarit. People, gods, poetry. A Sumerian text written by a student on clay tablets. According to the author, free variations on contemporary pessimistic phrases:

> *Where those sovereigns . . .*
> *no prosperity, no . . .*
> *how distant the sky, the hand . . .*
> *how deep the earth . . . no one knows*
> *life all a curse on your eyes*
> *joyless life if better than death*
> *for a single day of happiness*
> *pain . . . days and years, 36,000 in anguish*
> *on reaching the age appointed*
> *by God's will*
>
> *. . . . .*
> *what people do themselves is unknown*
> *their daily and nightly thoughts are known to God*
> *who does not burden people with work*
> *who does not speak ill of people*
> *who does not afflict the weak.*

The beggar goes before the fleet of foot
the rich man stretches out his hand to the pauper
such is the lot of the just
on reaching the age appointed
by God's will . . .

I have written down twenty minutes of the year. I have written down a little of my own life. Written it down. Down into the depths, into nonexistence, into Hades.

The beginning of the year is like a white sheet of paper. There has been a snowstorm during the night. I go out to beat the carpets. It is midday, but my footprints are the first outside the house. Perhaps something has happened, but nothing has yet reached us.

Like the sound of an axe-blow from the other side of the river.

Like the light of a new star from somewhere that is called 'above'. Although the sky is on every side: above, below, beside, behind and in front.

Here, too, as I have thought and spoken. And think and speak now, too. In the snowy sky. On the snowy ground. As life stands still like a clock that one has forgotten to wind.

The children are still sleeping after New Year's Eve.

The sheet of paper is still white. Silence is still silence.

The cloud is consoling to watch. Always.

Politics and politicians are gradually becoming streamlined, and in their streamlining uniform

like the newest cars, so similar that one has to look at what is written on the back to be certain which is a Toyota, which a Fiat, which a Ford, which a Renault.

Their wind resistance is always decreasing; headlights, windscreen wipers, aerials, door handles, principles and thoughts are concealed by the bodywork, which sinks closer to the ground,

consumes less petrol per 100 kilometres, weighs less and can, at the speed limit and without leaving traces or memories, race through the community, whose resistance and turbulence have been thoroughly examined on the test circuit.

In the beginning there is no content, only form, a round or square tin mould which stands on a high shelf in the cupboard and must be smeared with margarine, sprinkled with semolina, to make the content easier to extract.

You bake it for more than half an hour. Then, when a delicious smell begins to come from the oven, you use a knife to check that it is not doughy inside.

When it is ready, you take it carefully out of its tin. Then there is no more form, only content; and when the children have passed through the kitchen, not much of that, either.

What is lived in life becomes self.
For the self is a summary of life — space become time,
space which wants to exist in a larger space,
whose name is spring or heaven or love.
Then self can become creation.
To what purpose — perhaps no purpose at all.
Such is the flowing, and in this flowing
are we, our lives and thoughts,
meanings that arrive meaninglessly
like evening clouds in the sunset sky.
There can hardly be anything beyond it: space,
free space, free thought for all of us.

I ended up in literature because it seems, perhaps, closest to my proper place. But what is that proper place? It is that for which I seek, and do not find, a name. In fact, it may be that I do not seek it any longer, but seek instead the possibility of explaining to others that that place, that pigeonhole, does not really exist. It would be to compose poetry without being a poet; to write without being a writer; to philosophize without being a philosopher; to serve Christ without being a Christian; to serve Buddha without being a Buddhist; to express oneself without oneself being anyone.

Nouns are like ice and snow; in them is death and eternity, which are almost the same. Cold, icy, marmoreal eternity. Beauty, with a Capital Letter. Classical sculpture, which is now being destroyed, not by Christians and Muslims, but by the city air, that same city air which once made people free. I sometimes dream of a language in which there are no nouns, only verbs. A thought that may occur more easily to someone who knows the Finno-Ugrian languages, in which even negation is a verb. Like a remainder of an earlier living, changing and flowing world that gradually congeals, freezes into nouns, fossils, ice, theories, principles, and to which you try, more and more desperately and more and more resignedly, to speak of its own youth, of light, which is a flowing and a surging, and of life, which is light.

Behind the window, snow is falling, although it will soon be May; on the slope there are snowdrifts, and on a patch of ground that has been cleared of snow, numb with cold, robins and hedge-sparrows peck at oatflakes. At the same time terribly close and terribly distant. The gaze of the robin's black eye will reach me perhaps only when I, never mind the robin, no longer exist. Perhaps my gaze will also reach him, but it is not certain. For the present, I shall try to speak in words. To speak of life, which cannot be contained in words, which cannot be explained or understood, which can only be lived, and perhaps also protected, like this robin, which is watching me, head tilted, from the top of the little pine, from a couple of decades of light years, or life years — life is the light of men — away.

Time dies away. Or melts away. There is still a little time on the north side of the house, under the eaves, on the edge of the forest and under the forest. But in the sunlight it becomes watery and fragile and retreats. Only a little dampness remains, which in the sunlight soon dries, among the molehills and bluebells and anemones, slowly unfurling themselves.

There is still something that remains; yesterday morning early it was like a mist over the pond and marsh, but today by midday it has become a blue-green haze that floats above the forest and will clear over a few days, so that finally nothing is left but a shimmer of air on the field and the ripple of a skylark somewhere high above. I believe that what remains is eternity.

TV. The weather. At night, temperatures between 1° and 6° are expected, ground temperatures between 0° and -3° in places.

Children. Dirty, smelling of dust and sunshine, sleepy. One stays up to watch the TV news and refuses to go to bed, although it is close to midnight.

Toys. They, too, are dirty. The white bears, Hidy and Howdy, are grey again; they need to be washed again.

Associations and midges fly around, sometimes inside, sometimes outside, behind the half-open door, where it is so quiet that the crackling of the bonfire in a distant garden reaches me here. I watch: flames and smoke rise vertically upward. Around the fire my neighbours – father and son – busy themselves. In the evening sky, clouds are forming for tomorrow – although it will be no surprise if they have disappeared by morning – and further away, in the coppice behind the ponds, two nightingales are singing. On the bookshelves, where there is no more space, some books lie crossways on top of others.

Estonian villages in the Nineteenth Century.
Estonian villages in the Nineteenth Century.

Under the table are a small knife, three pencils and a lorry.

Three red tulips are going out in the darkness like flames. Perhaps they should be put to bed for the night, as fire used to be put to bed. And in the morning, be wakened like fire. Life-fire. For life is fire, burning, only very slow. We burn for seventy years, or, if we are very strong, eighty; a good fire will consume us in a couple of hours. The whole Jewish race, the Estonian race or the population of Hamburg can be burned away in a few years, as was attempted in my childhood. Today it could undoubtedly be achieved much more quickly.

So I sit here, behind me my neighbours' yellow bonfire in the garden and in front the red flame of the tulips, which has almost melted into the darkness. My eyes can hardly any longer make out the red colour or the letters on the page. What I have just written is laboured and sorrowful.

Naturally I did not wish or intend to speak of this. Rather, this day, this life and fire, are like a glass dome or a gong or a bell, which rings for long, for long. Sometimes it is difficult to say when or if that ringing will ever end, or whether it will trap all other sounds, and transform them into its own voice, ringing on forever, as if it were the most essential thing of all, as if it fulfilled the command of someone with whom we cannot succeed in communicating in any language but the ringing that traps and transforms echoes, but that apparently has no significance at all.

That ringing, too, is like life. Like fire. Which, then, is the older, fire or sound? Or meaning, the fact that one thing stands in the place of another; is another, is and is not. Perhaps, then, also they. Perhaps, then, also we. Perhaps, then, also these words here.

I came from the town. I fetched some cucumber and flower seedlings from my neighbour; put the flowers into the larder to keep cool; planted the cucumbers and sowed some pepper seeds I had brought from the town in the greenhouse, watered them, cut the flourishing grass, nettles and dandelions from around the young apple trees; and then felt sweaty and tired, went down to the lake, took off my clothes and swam. The weather was hot, nearly 25°. I sat, naked, on a bench for a moment and listened to the nightingales. We have not had any for many years, but now, by the lake, where the great weeping willows and bird cherries grow, one had appeared, which, unperturbed by either me or the daylight, did nothing but warble, chuck, and gurgle – clearly a great talent among its kind. Then my glance fell on the bird cherry blossoms which covered the ground around the bench. This year there had not been the usual cold spell when the bird cherry flowered. I thought about this, and suddenly there came to my mind something which I had noticed, but which was waiting somewhere on the borders of consciousness for further attention: earlier, when I had been speaking with the neighbour's wife, there had been some bird cherry blossom in her hair. Now that I had dealt with it, I began to feel better: one fact would leave me in peace, would no longer demand a reaction. We had met, I had nodded to it, clearly I was no longer of any use to it. The bird-cherry blossoms simply let me go. But they were not, and are not, definitely alone. Definitely, my mind is full of such impressions and notes awaiting and demanding attention. It is as if an alarm bell were constantly ringing somewhere, you are restless, without yourself knowing why; you have simply forgotten, perhaps deliberately, perhaps accidentally, the queue of unconscious things behind the doors of your consciousness.

Autumn comes closer. Everything drowns in yellow.
Golden rod and dahlia. For many months
you had lost your voice; now you begin to chime
more purely and more clearly. In a minor key.
And the yellow, the yellow is every day
fuller of bees, flies and remembrance
of childhood gardens in Tartu and Pärnu,
which were just as languid, luxuriant and damp
and full of the same stillness
in which grasshoppers play music with your soul
and the great hawk moth, which you find
each morning under the well cover,
knocks each night at the window,
longing to come closer to the lamp
by whose light you sit and write
and think that in autumn borders begin to disappear
leaving moods and colours
leaving the yellow, the yellow . . .

Restlessness lives in peace,
like a white dot in a black circle,
like a black dot in a white circle.

For some time a car has been rattling
behind the hill on to the road, surely
it is trapped. The crickets are silent.
Peace does not live in restlessness.
In the western sky is a yellowish streak.
There is no bridge, no hair-fine
grasshopper song of the chord,
no flimsy bridge
to the other side.

A mouse climbs up the wall of the attic room
and runs across the ceiling.
Then comes silence, and in the silence
my own inner cricket
begins to chirr,
the one I learned to hear
as a child, on my sickbed
when I took my first steps
along the taut string
away from my own fevered body
into timelessness, spacelessness, voice.

I come up from the cellar: suddenly everything is full of light.

The light greets everything, greets the flower-vase and smiles at it, greets the teddy bear, me and the torch high on the shelf.

The light caresses the backs of all the books at once and shines on all the specks of dust at once, and the dust begins to dance.

The light reminds us, all us specks of dust, that redemption is the understanding that you are redeemed; understanding is the understanding that you have not understood.

Is not and *is* – between them runs the thinnest of thin lines: it has no thickness, no colour, no smell or weight.

Through it? But that is the same as if nothing happened. The spot of sunlight on the wall reaches the seam between two pieces of wallpaper and the cherry petal comes loose from the blossom and begins to fall, continues falling;

for us, in our time, it will never reach the ground, will never find redemption, will never decay.

But in its own time it reaches the floor, finds redemption and understanding.

Is there a third time, something outside past and future (it is not the present, the present is nothing but the border between them), which unites it and our own time, understanding, decay and redemption,

which for a moment wipes away the line between *is not* and *is* like the light whose smile set the dust in the room dancing?

A bird in the air. It is not its wings that bear its wings. Its wings are borne by the air. Words stand on wordlessness, logic on the absence of logic.

But sometimes we are, after all, closer to what exists. Before there is something that is like a blanket on top of one who sleeps. The body is unknown, but the blanket has its own folds, bumps and hollows.

We know someone is there beneath the blanket, but that "someone" and that "knowing" and that "we" are even more under wraps than what is under the blanket. We are the blanket, not the sleeper.

We do not know whether he is alive or dead, although from time to time it looks as if he is breathing. And a blanket cannot breathe.

So it is not all the same, after all; all is not a game. But playing is allowed under the blanket, too – hide-and-seek, and make-believe that you are a badger in its sett or a fox in its lair.

I try to speak of this. Always. To think. Sleeping and waking. But my voice resounds as though from deep underwater, and nothing reaches the surface but bubbles.

Truth itself is also a bubble, which you build laboriously there beneath the water's surface, like a water spider, which builds itself a nest and drags air into it, bubble by bubble.

The nest looks like a little silver ball, like a globule of quicksilver, at once so heavy and so agile.

Truth is a bubble, part of the Truth which saves us from suffocating. Truth is that which breathes, and allows others to breathe.

In the room, a moth flies from east to west: here inside, too, east and west exist, in the room, in the matchbox and the eye of the needle.

A child throws an orange pip at the window. Bicycles – big and small – lie in each other's embrace in the year's last snow, the year's last freedom,

in which mirrors make themselves transparent, traversable as rooms

in which bricks become mirrors in which you see the moth's shadow on your face,

which looks, like the god Janus, at once to east and west, forward and back, and sees the orange-pip at once falling and rising.

I have no principles.
In my depths are no thoughts.
In the depths is clear water that flows
in the dimness over stones, a few shells or caddis fly,
minnows
and roach,
water-moss and speedwells
that tremble in the current
like the strings of an instrument, only unheard.
At the bottom of the stream are no thoughts,
only flowing, only the current's
categorical imperative
which bends and bows with it
the mosses and speedwells, the fish and caddis flies,
teaching some to cling to the stones on the bottom,
others to the flowing water itself,
which is called swimming.

In the ventilation grating lives a titmouse.
Couperin lives at this moment on the gramophone.
Tadpoles are already living in the pond.
Above the pond, at evening, is a mist, and in the mist live
    nightingales.
As long as they are there, as they come back in springtime,
there is still order and hope in the world, there are still the
    frail threads of migration paths
that connect us with Egypt, Sudan, the Congo, and Cape
    Province.
The world is still in place, like a map-mosaic, a children's
    puzzle, a jigsaw,
that is so hard to put together and so easy to break up.
My greatest fear is, indeed, perhaps that the time will come
    when some of the pieces of the mosaic will disappear:
the nightingales will not come, the dung-beetle will not fly,
    and it will no longer be possible to put the world together
    again.
It will remain a confused, half-finished ecological puzzle:
a solitary titmouse will sing, but will not find a mate.
In the ocean the male blue whale will no longer find his
    partner.
The continents will break up into islets, skerries, stones
    surrounded by water.
Mankind will break up into parties, classes, principles, homos
    and sapiens,
naked apes which fear serpents, the dark, knowledge and other
    such things
and cower each by his own swaying coconut palm, trying to
    piece together his own map of the stars,
which scatters into the mist like everything else.
The titmouse came back again. The nightingale is singing.

NOTES

page

9   *Metal is easily dug into the ground*: an example of Soviet Wastefulness.

15   *The Estonian time*: the period of Estonian independence, 1918–39.
     Tin crowns were placed on new graves.

19   *Gunnar Ekelöf* (1907–68): Swedish poet. (English translation of
     Ekelöf's poem by David McDuff).

26   *Harry Martinson*: (1904–78): Swedish poet.

27   *Pond Hill . . . Southern and Northern Kingdoms*: Mounds of earth at
     our pond; our children's playground.

28   *Kantele*: a Finno-Ugrian zither-like folk instrument.

35   *Radar*: in the Soviet period, a military airport was located close
     to Tartu.

35   *Linnaea borealis*: twinflower.

36   *Juhan Liiv* (1864–1913) *and Paul-Erik Rummo* (b. 1942): Estonian
     poets.

40   *Ostyak language*: Finn-Ugric language spoken by the Ostyak
     people living in the basin of the River Ob in western Siberia.

44   *Raccoon dog*: raccoon-like wild dog (*Nyctereutes*), originating
     in Eastern Asia.

49   *Forest Brethren*: Estonian nationalist partisans active after the
     Second World War.

52, 59   *Saaremaa, Muhu*: islands off the northwestern coast of Estonia.

59   *Kalevala*: the Finnish national epic.

59   *Norbert Wiener* (1894–1964): US mathematician and philosopher,
     inventor of cybernetics.

59   *The song of the Chukchi*: a people who live in northeastern-
     most Russia.

63   *Eppur si viene*: But it does come. Galileo's famous reply to the
     Inqustion's assertion that the movement of the earth round
     the sun had yet to be scientifically proved was: *Eppur si muove*
     (But it does move).

64   *The bridge of Cinvat*: The razor-thin bridge to the world of the
     dead in ancient Iranian mythology.

64   *Halmahera Island*: An ancient island in Indonesia.

67   *Paal-Helge Haugen* (b. 1945): Norwegian poet.

71   *Eastern European time*: Estonia moved to Eastern European time
     when it gained its independence in 1991.

71   *Ugarit*: Ancient Syrian city-state on the Mediterranean coast.